What Am I?

Steve Chasteen

A WHITELEY PRESS, LLC, BOOK

A Whiteley Press, LLC, Book
www.bectonliterary.com

ISBN: 9798324292324

This book is dedicated
to all the dogs
who need a family to love.

Hello!

My name is Callie Callaisienne.

Can you guess what I am?

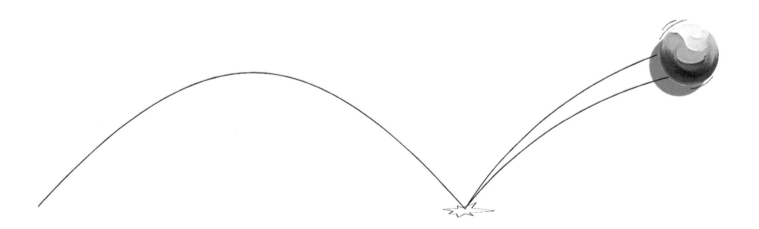

I have a nose.

Am I a cat?

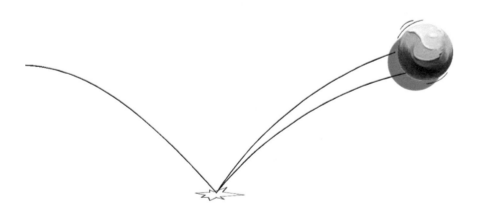

No!

I am not a cat.

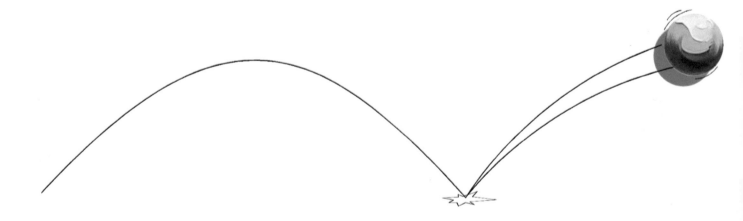

I have two ears.

Am I a rabbit?

No!

I am not a rabbit.

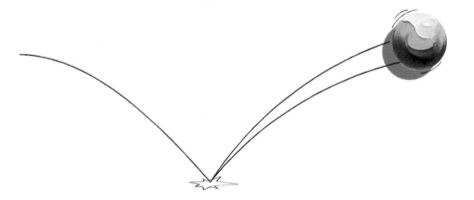

I have two brown eyes.

Am I a fox?

No!

I am not a fox.

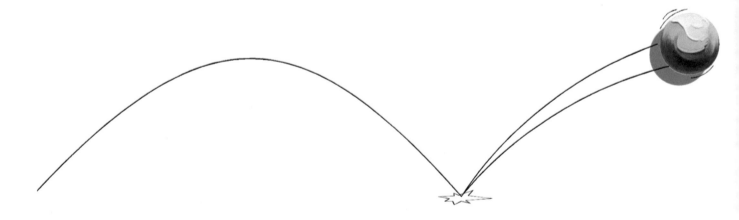

I have a pretty face.

Am I an actress?

No!

I am not an actress.

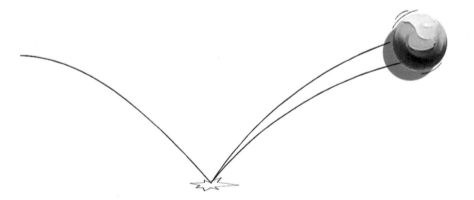

I have a tail.

Am I a fish?

No!

I am not a fish.

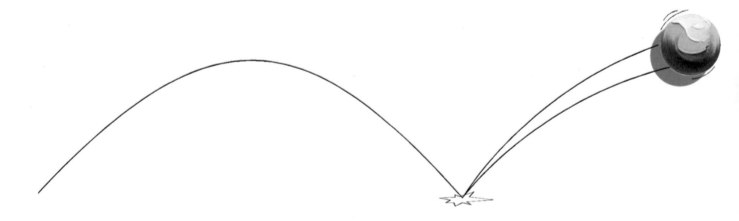

I have four feet.

Am I a pig?

No!

I am not a pig.

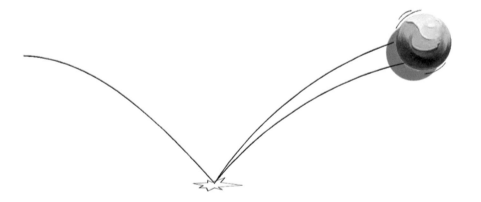

I love to run everywhere.

Am I a squirrel?

No!

I am not a squirrel.

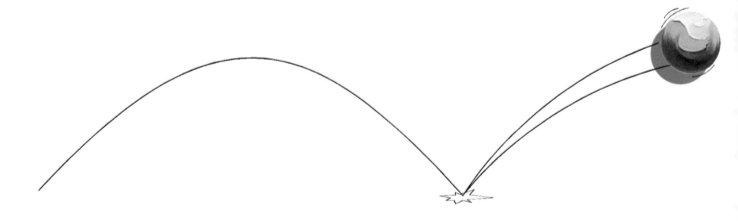

I have black fur.

Am I a black bear?

No!

I am not a black bear.

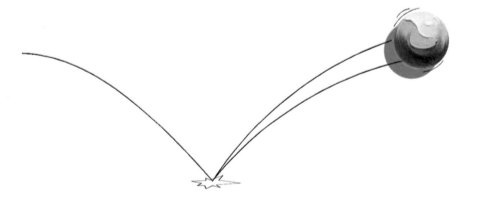

I love wagging my tail
when my family comes home.

Am I a dog?

Yes!

My name is Callie Callaisienne!
A pretty dog! I am eleven years
old.

I live in Calais, and I love my
family because they gave me a
wonderful home when I was
young.

I am very happy at home!

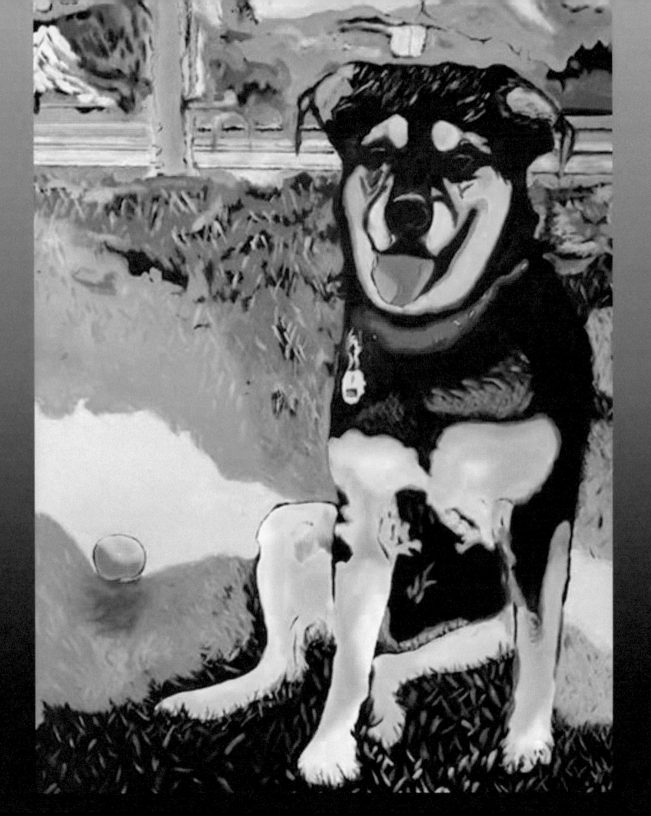

Hello, my friends!

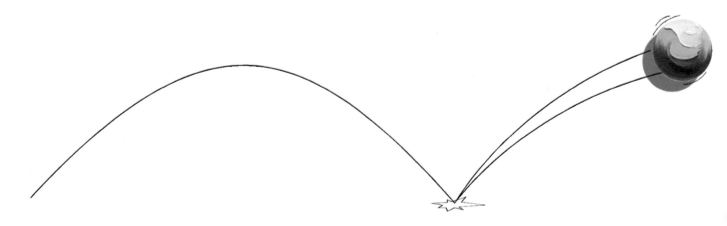

The End.

ABOUT THE AUTHOR

Steve Chasteen is a first-time author who loves animals, people, and especially children...their boundless desire to learn and the innocent joy they give so freely. He lives near Atlanta, Georgia, with his wife of 44 years and loves his daughter and her dog Callie very much.

He loves fly fishing, backpacking, and oil painting. That's his painting of Callie on the last page.

WATCH FOR

BOOK 2

COMING SOON!

Romans 8:28

Made in the USA
Columbia, SC
21 July 2024

38970385R00018